UNDERSTANDING PEOPLE IN

The Vikings

MARGARET HUDSON

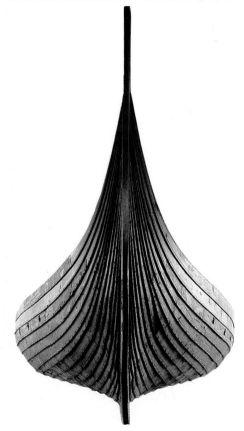

First published in Great Britain by
Heinemann Library
an imprint of Heinemann Publishers
(Oxford) Ltd
Halley Court, Jordan Hill, Oxford OX2 8EJ

OXFORD LONDON EDINBURGH MADRID
ATHENS BOLOGNA PARIS MELBOURNE
SYDNEY AUCKLAND SINGAPORE TOKYO
IBADAN NAIROBI HARARE GABORONE
PORTSMOUTH NH (USA)

© 1994 Heinemann Library

98 97 96 95 94
10 9 8 7 6 5 4 3 2 1

**British Library Cataloguing in Publication
Data is available from the British Library
on request.**

ISBN 0 431 07801 7 (hardback)
       0 431 07782 7 (paperback)

Designed by Ron Kamen, Green Door
Design Ltd, Basingstoke

Printed in China

Photographic acknowledgements
The author and publishers wish to
acknowledge with thanks the following
photographic sources:

a = above b = below l = left r = right

Arnamagneaan Institute, Reykjavik p11; A.
T. A. Stockholm pp9, 14, 49, 57; ARXIU-
MAS, Barcelona p52; Bibliothek der
Rijksuniversiteit, Utrech p53; Copenhagen
University p27b; C. M. Dixon pptitle, 5a,
81l, and r, 10, 13, 15a, 17a and b, 18, 20a,
21, 25a, 27a, 29, 32, 33b, 42, 47a, 48, 56, 58;
Werner Forman Archive titlel page pp12
(statens Historiska Museet, Stockholm), 15b
(National Museum of Iceland), 16a, (Statens
Historiska Museet, Stockholm), 16b, (Manz
Museum), 26 (National Museum,
Copenhagen), 35b (Statens Historiska
Museet, Stockholm), 59a and cover and b;
Robert Harding Photograph Library pp45,
54b; Historic Scotland, Edinburgh pp9b, 60;
Historiska Museet, Stockholm p30; Michael
Holford pp20b, 28; Kungl Biblioteket,
Stockholm p44; National Museet,
Copenhagen pp24, 43b; National Museum
of Ireland p51; Roskilde Museum, Denmark
p7a, Scottish Tourist Board pp19, 50;
Stofnun Arna Magnussonar, Reykjavik
p54a; Trustees of the National Museums of
Scotland p39a; Historisk Museum,
Universitetet 1, Bergen p7a; University
Museum of National Antiquities, Oslo pp5b
(photograph Eirik I Johnsen); 23a, 24, 25b,
33a, 37a and b, 39 and cover 43a and cover
and b; Weidenfeld and Nicolson Archive 51,
57; York Archaeological Trust pp6, 7b, 22,
23b, 36b.

The publishers have made every effort to
trace the copyright holders, but if they
have inadvertently overlooked any, they
will be pleased to make the necessary
arrangement at the first opportunity.

Cover photograph © Pierpont Morgan
Library

Note to the reader – In this book there are some words in the text which are printed in **bold** type. This shows that the word is lited in the glossary on page 62. The glossary gives a brief explanation of words which may be new to you.

Contents

Who were the Vikings?

The Vikings lived about a thousand years ago. They came from the area that is now Norway, Denmark and Sweden. People called them Northmen, or Norsemen, then Vikings. Why did the name change?

In their language 'viking' meant both 'to travel' and 'a pirate raid'. The Vikings did both. They sailed all over much of the known world. The first that many peoples knew of the Vikings was when they came to raid their lands.

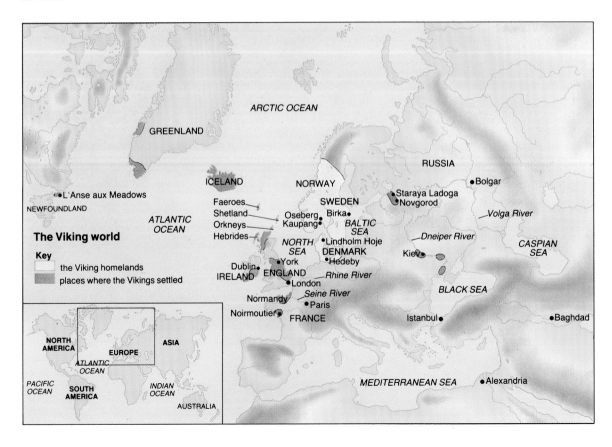

The Viking world

Key

☐ the Viking homelands
■ places where the Vikings settled

Why did the Vikings do this? There were several reasons:

1 The lands they lived in had very little good farming land, and the number of people living there was growing. They needed to find new land to farm. At first, they raided places, but later they came back to settle there.

2 The Vikings were great traders. They wanted to find new lands to trade with.

3 The ideas of adventuring and raiding were built into their way of life. They expected to do it.

A silver brooch
The Vikings were clever at making things. They made many things to trade.

Part of a Viking ship
They needed ships for both raiding and trading.

The Vikings behaved in the same way in almost all of the lands they found. If they found a country with no one living there, like Iceland when they found it, they settled there. If there were people living there, like Scotland when they found it, they traded with them, or took what they wanted without trading, or both. Later they spent the winter in these countries, then settled there to farm.

How we know about the Vikings 1

The best way to find out about the Vikings is to look at things from their time which still exist today. These could be buildings, ships, graves or **artefacts** (objects which they have made, such as combs, bowls or clothes). Most of these were buried, or even built over, as time has passed. Places where Vikings lived may be under modern cities – like York. Other place may have been ploughed up, or just worn away by time and the weather.

Archaeologists in York in 1979
They have dug down to the right layers of soil for the Vikings. They look for changes in the colour of the soil. This shows where wooden posts or rubbish pits were. Finding posts tells us what houses were like. Rubbish pits show us what they threw away. This tells us about what they ate and drank, and also about their belongings. Archaeologists found beads, keys, knives, brooches, coins and even shoes here.

An early Viking grave in Westness, in the Orkneys
The way that people were buried tells us about their religion and what things were important to them. This man was buried with weapons, farming tools and pieces for a board game.

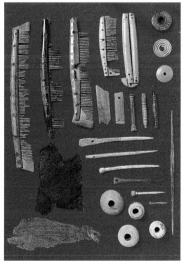

Some things found in York
The combs and pins were made from bone or animal horn.

Viking sites have been **excavated** by **archaeologists**, who dig down, layer by layer. They excavate slowly, and they make drawings and take photographs as they go. The further down they dig the further back in time they get. Viking buildings and other remains can tell us a lot about how the Vikings lived and what they believed.

We can find out a lot about the Vikings from the stories they told. To begin with, stories, histories or poems were not written down, but spoken and learned.

In the 1100s the Vikings in Iceland began to write them down, on animal skins. Some of these writings were meant to be accurate. Others, like the **sagas**, mixed fact and fiction.

These carvings tell the story of Sigurd, Dragon Slayer.

2 ▶
Killing the dragon

◀ 4
Fighting over the treasure

◀ 3
Roasting the dragon's heart

1 ▶
Making a sword

f u t h a r k h n i a s t b m l R

Runes

The first Vikings wrote by carving on wood, bone and stone. They had to have an alphabet with only a few curves. The letters they worked out are called **runes**. At first there were 26 runes, but these were cut down to the 16 runes in the box on the left.

The runes in the picture are carved on the long, thin body of the dragon. They say: 'Sigrid built this bridge in memory of her husband, Holmer. She was Orm's daughter.'

We can also find out about the Vikings from what other people at the time wrote about them. Many of these people, such as English monks, had been raided by Vikings. They may not have written about them fairly.

This gameboard was carved on a stone in Buckquoy, Orkneys. It shows that the Vikings enjoyed games.

Society and government

There were three main groups in Viking society. The diagram below shows what they were.

Jarls: earls, rich landowners

Karls: free men

Thralls: slaves

A modern photograph of Tynwald Hill, on the Isle of Man. The Vikings settled in the Isle of Man and brought their ways of running things there. The Isle of Man still has a meeting of its own parliament here every year. They do this because this was where the Things were always held.

Free men could become slaves if they lost land. Slaves could buy freedom and become free men. Earls and free men met regularly to discuss problems and settle disputes. These meetings were called **Things**.

At first, a king was just the most powerful earl. As kings took more power, Things only dealt with local problems. The kings made the big decisions.

Iceland never had a king. It had local Things, like everywhere else, but the big decisions were made at an Althing, a Thing for all free men all over Iceland, which was held for two weeks each year.

Vikings obeyed the laws that were made by kings or Things. These laws were known to everyone. If someone refused to obey the laws they were **outlawed** from the Thing. They could not farm any land. No one could help them or feed them. They lived in hiding, and they had to steal to eat.

Pages from a saga or story about Harold Finehair
He was the first king to rule most of the area called Norway on the map. He is in many sagas, including the *Orkney Saga*, because he raided Orkney and Scotland.

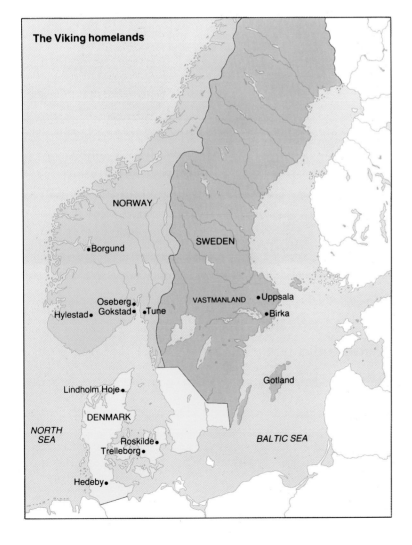

The Viking homelands

NORWAY

SWEDEN

Borgund

Oseberg
Hylestad• Gokstad• •Tune

VASTMANLAND •Uppsala
•Birka

Gotland

Lindholm Hoje•

DENMARK

NORTH
SEA

Roskilde•
Trelleborg•

BALTIC SEA

Hedeby•

This map shows more or less where the Viking homelands were. The edges of each area changed from time to time. The Vikings did not have this much space to live in. They could not grow crops on most of the land, because it was not very good.

Clothes and appearance

Viking clothes were made to be comfortable and sensible. The styles hardly changed for hundreds of years.

The picture on page 13 shows the kinds of clothes Vikings wore. This does not mean that everyone wore exactly the same things. Most clothes were made by the women of the family at home. If the women were good at making clothes, they could be well decorated or quite complicated. If the women were not good at making clothes, they would be more simple.

This Viking pendant shows how women dressed. The dress is pleated and the woman has a shawl over it. She has long hair.

The women spun the wool (or flax for linen) and then wove it into cloth. Then they dyed the cloth with vegetable dyes, because they liked to wear bright colours. Vegetable dyes could be used to make lots of different colours – yellow, black, green, brown, blue and red. Then they made clothes from the cloth. It was a long job, so people did not have many clothes. The clothes they had needed to last a long time.

This is how a Viking farmer/warrior and his wife would have dressed.

Most Viking men and women had long hair. Some of them plaited their hair to keep it out of the way. Others held it back with a scarf (if they were women) or headband (if they were men). Both men and women wore jewellery. Travellers at the time report that some men and women wore eye make-up as well.

A Viking brooch
Viking women wore brooches like this one, in pairs, to hold up their tunics.

Family life

Vikings lived in family groups. Parents, children, grandparents, aunts and cousins all counted as part of the family. They were loyal to each other. If someone harmed a member of a Viking family, the whole family went to the Thing to ask for the wrong to be put right.

If a man was killed, his family asked for money or land to make up for his death. If the Thing said they should be paid, and if the murderer (or his family) paid up, then it was over. If the family felt the Thing had been unfair, or if the murderer or his family did not pay, then the family of the murdered man killed someone from the murderer's family. This family would then kill someone from the other family, and so on. This was called a feud. Feuds could last many years.

A girl's marriage was often fixed by her family, but she had the chance to turn down at least one man they picked. Once she was married she kept her own property, and looked after her husband's land when he was away.

The runes carved on this stone are about Odindisa, the wife of a farmer from Hassmyra in Sweden. It praises her for caring for the farm and her family.

Divorce was easy. The husband or wife had to make a speech, in front of witnesses, to explain why they wanted a divorce. This was all they had to do. Some of the reasons given for divorce seem odd now. One man divorced his wife because she wore trousers instead of a dress.

Viking children lived at home until they were in their teens, when they went to live with another family. Boys learnt how to farm and fight and sail. They also learned how to make tools and weapons. Girls learnt how to fight, too. They learned how to spin and weave, and make butter and cheese.

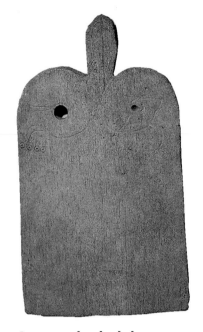

A carved whalebone board
Historians think these boards were used for ironing clothes.

The Vikings played lots of different board games. Lots of them were games of attack and defence, good practice for battles. In this game, one side has a king, which it has to keep safe. The other side has to capture the king.

Viking gods

The Viking believed in lots of different gods and goddesses. These gods all looked after different parts of daily life. They could appear on earth and make things happen. Many of them, such as Woden and Thor, were like the gods and goddesses of the Saxons.

A charm shaped like Thor's hammer

Vikings gods were said to live in a place called Asgard. Like Heaven, Asgard was somewhere above the clouds. Earth was called Midgard. Below earth was Niflheim, a cold misty place, which was the Viking idea of Hell.

The Vikings thought that if a Viking died in battle he would go to a special hall in Asgard called Valhalla. Here they would feast, sing and tell stories. If they died in their beds they would go to Niflheim.

This carved stone from the Isle of Man shows Ragnarok. This was the Viking story of the end of the world.

Because the Vikings thought that people went somewhere else when they died, they buried people with things they might need on the journey. They gave them food, clothes, tools and even, in the case of a famous warrior or a king, a ship to sail in.

Viking beliefs

As well as believing in gods and goddesses, the Vikings believed in many other creatures which could be good or bad. They believed in goblins, trolls and ghosts.

The Vikings also believed that there were special people who could tell the future. They called these people soothsayers. Here is a description of a visit from a soothsayer, from the saga of Eric the Red:

Thorkell asked a wise woman to his house. Before she came everyone ran about to get things ready just as she wanted. He had a high chair set out, with a cushion stuffed with chicken feathers. As soon as she arrived she asked the women to help her sing a magic song, then she got ready all she needed and said: 'There are many spirits here, and they have told me things I did not know before.' Then everyone went up to her in turn and she told them what they wanted to know. In almost every case the things she said would happen did come true.

A model of Thor, the god of thunder

Living on the land

Most Vikings were farmers. They did not live in towns. There were a few big trading ports, such as York and Birka, but most Vikings lived on small farms in family groups.

We can find out what these farms were like by reading the sagas and looking at farms that have been excavated. Farms were all built in a similar way. The main building was an oblong longhouse, where the family lived and worked (see pages 22–3). Sometimes there was just a longhouse, which the family shared with the animals. People added more buildings to their farms as time went on. Around the longhouse were smaller buildings for animals and a **smithy**, where the farmers made their tools and weapons.

Iceland had little wood or stone, so houses were built very long and low. They had roofs made of turf (blocks of grass and earth). This kept the heat in in winter. Sometimes the whole house was built of turf.

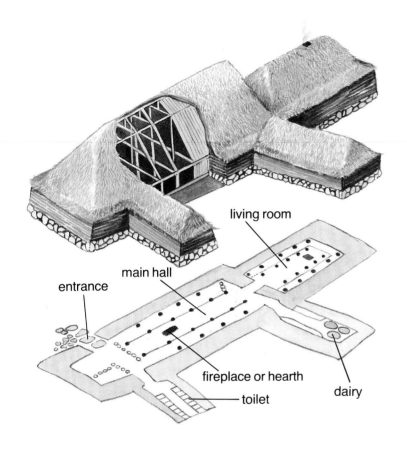

living room

main hall

entrance

fireplace or hearth

toilet

dairy

A farmhouse at Stöng, Iceland

It was 17 m long by 6 m wide. The toilet was also a bath-house, where the people had steam baths. In the first room after the entrance, before the main hall, there was a fireplace to cook on. This room was also a store. The women used to spin and weave in the living room.

The photograph and line drawing below show the farm at Jarlshof, in the Shetlands, Scotland.

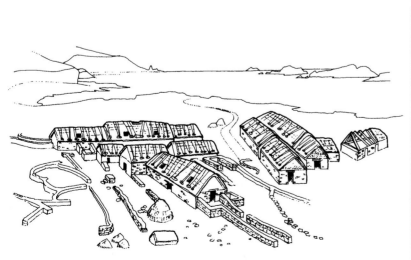

The farming year

Most farms were quite small, and were farmed by the family. Larger farms needed more workers. The farmers could hire free men who had no land, or could buy slaves to do the work.

Farming followed the pattern it still follows today. Seeds were sown in spring, and the crops were harvested in the late summer.

In the autumn, animals that could not be fed through the winter were killed. The meat from them was smoked, dried or stored in salt to make it keep longer, without going bad.

This carving shows a man fishing with a spear. They used nets and hooks, too.

The pictures running along the bottom of this tapestry show farming methods that are very like Viking ones.

20

In spring Svein worked hard to sow the seeds. As soon as this work was done, he went a-viking and raided the Scottish islands. He came home in mid-summer for the harvest, then went a-viking until winter fell.
From the *Orkney Saga*

Farmers were raiders, too. Raiding fitted in around the farming year. As the saga above says, many farmers went raiding twice a year, after the sowing and the harvesting. While they were gone their wives ran the farms and made sure that everything was done at the right time.

The winter weather was too bad for the Vikings to farm or to raid. They stayed indoors mending tools, making clothes and cleaning the skins of the animals that had been killed. They also got their ships ready for the next year.

Most farmers made their own tools and weapons. Most of these would have been very simple. There were some people who made their living by skills other than farming. Some of them made weapons and tools. The tools these people made were more decorated, like the axe head shown above.

Inside a longhouse

In the earliest longhouses, there was just one long room where the whole family lived, ate and slept. They shared it with the animals. Longhouses could be as long as 40 m, although most of them were about 20 m (see page 19).

The longhouse had benches built down the sides. People sat on these in the daytime and slept on them at night. The benches often had spaces under them for storing clothes and bedding. There would be one 'high chair' for the most important person in the family and his wife. There was sometimes another 'high chair' for important visitors.

A reconstruction of a longhouse in York
The fire was in the middle of the longhouse. It was often the only place for cooking and keeping warm.

Longhouses were probably dark and damp. The floor was just earth. If the walls were made of turf they had wooden walls built inside, if possible, with a gap between the wall and the turf, to stop the wood from rotting. Sometimes a longhouse had two doors. Only a few longhouses had windows with shutters that could be closed at night. Most only got light from the doors and the hole in the roof which was supposed to let out the smoke from the fire. Other light came from candles made of animal fat. These were smoky and smelly.

A wooden bed
Its owner must have been very important, because most people slept on benches or sleeping platforms.

Viking women spun and wove the cloth for their clothes. The woman in this reconstruction in York is spinning wool on a spindle. She spins the spindle, and pulls the wool gently from the clump in her hand. The spindle twists the wool. After the wool was spun it was often dyed bright colours. Then it was woven on a loom like the one in the picture.

Cooking and eating

Archaeologists have found lots of evidence in homes and rubbish pits to show what the Vikings ate, and how they cooked it.

The Vikings ate a lot of meat and fish. They kept pigs for their meat. They kept chickens, geese and ducks for their eggs and for meat. They kept cows, sheep and goats for their milk and for meat. They also hunted wild animals for meat, and caught and ate a great deal of fish. The Vikings grew rye and barley for bread. They ate a lot of cabbages and onions. They used many different herbs and flavourings, which they found growing wild, such as garlic and cress. They drank beer, milk, water and a drink made from honey.

The Vikings ate two main meals a day, at about eight in the morning and seven at night. They all ate together, with the master of the house and his wife sitting in the 'high chair'.

Some cooking equipment from the Viking period
Most Viking eating and cooking equipment was made of wood, except, of course, for the pots that hung over the fire. This picture shows a Viking dish, knife, bucket and large ladle.

What a Viking cooking hearth was like

The big pots were stood on iron stands with three legs, or hung from the ceiling over the fire. The cauldrons were filled with meat and vegetables. Other things could be hung over the sides of the cauldron to cook in the steam. Food could also be cooked on hot stones in the fire itself. Some farmhouses, like the one at Jarlshof in the Shetlands, had stone ovens, too.

The Vikings used plates and bowls made of wood. They had knives and spoons but no forks. They drank from wooden cups, or out of hollowed out animal horns.

These are some of the things that the Vikings took with them when they went on journeys. Some of these things would be needed on the journey, others would be needed when they landed.

Viking storytelling

The Vikings enjoyed storytelling and poetry. For a long time the only way that they had of passing on tales of their history or their legends was by telling them as stories. There were people whose job it was to remember the old stories and to make up new ones. It would have taken a very long time to tell a story by carving runes on stones or bones!

The Vikings told each other stories during the long winter months indoors. They also had three festivals when they had feasts. People travelled a long way to these feasts. They would bring their best clothes to wear. Then the poems and stories were said by a Viking who told stories for a living.

The storytellers also went to weddings and rich Vikings' halls. At these feasts there was singing and dancing. Viking singing seemed to take some time to get used to – an Arab trader who visited Hedeby, in Denmark, said: 'I have never heard more horrible singing. It's like dogs barking, only much nastier.'

Storytellers were often given presents, like this ring, after a feast. Sagas and poems often seem boastful to us now, because the Vikings felt that it was right to list all the things that you could do. So Kali Kolsson, in the *Orkney Saga*, a history written in Iceland around 1200, says:

I am clever at these:
A champion at chess,
I get my runes right,
I can write and read.
I am a skillful skier,
rower, and bowman.
And more, master
Of music and poetry.

One summer King Harald Finehair sailed west against the Vikings who raided his kingdom and spent their winters in the Orkneys and the Shetlands. He took control of the Shetlands, Orkneys and the Hebrides. When he returned to Norway he gave control of the Orkneys and the Shetlands to Earl Rögnvald, to compensate him for the death of his son, who was killed fighting for Harald. Earl Rögnvald gave them, in turn, to Earl Sigurd, who then ruled them until his death.

Part of the *Orkney Saga*. As it is a saga, things will have been changed to make a better story.

This is a picture from a seventeenth century edition of *Egil's Saga*. This saga told the story of Egil's family.

The Vikings liked playing with words. Sagas were full of *kennings*, which were ways of describing something without using its name. For example, a sword would be called 'a battle adder'. They also enjoyed riddles. Sometimes the riddle would be part of a saga, but they also liked swapping riddles in the same way that we tell jokes now.

Sport and games

Most of the games that the Vikings enjoyed were sports where they competed with each other. They liked horse racing, rowing, sailing and swimming. They liked to watch and take part in wrestling matches. Often they had a special place for these matches. It was a flat field with a pointed stone in the middle called the wrestling stone. The wrestlers tried to force each other onto the stone.

Hunting, skiing and skating were sports that were also important skills. Hunting provided fresh meat. In winter it was hard to walk or ride. Skiing and skating got them further.

This scene from the Bayeux Tapestry shows people out hunting with hawks and dogs.

Many Viking sports, such as wrestling, weightlifting, shooting with bows and arrows and running, were seen as training to prepare a man to be a good warrior. Many of the games that they played indoors in the winter months were also seen this way. Most of their board games were about working out ways to capture each other.

Vikings also spent time making toys for their children. Some of them were simple wooden shapes, others were more complicated. At Jarlshof, in the Shetlands, archaeologists found a toy stone quern (querns were used to grind corn) which really worked.

These Viking chess pieces were found on the Isle of Lewis in the Hebrides. The Viking probably learned chess from the Arabs, with whom they traded. It was the kind of game they enjoyed, where they had to work out battle tactics.

The port of Birka

Although most Vikings lived on farms they also needed some places where they could all go to trade. There were several ports all around the lands the Vikings settled in, and these became important trading places. York was one of them. The town of Birka, on lake Malar in Sweden, was another.

At first these ports were quite small. Traders came to them at certain times and set up stalls to trade. Then they went home.

Trading went on at Birka all year round. In summer ships could sail into the port. In winter the lake froze, but the traders still came, on skates or sledges, over the ice.

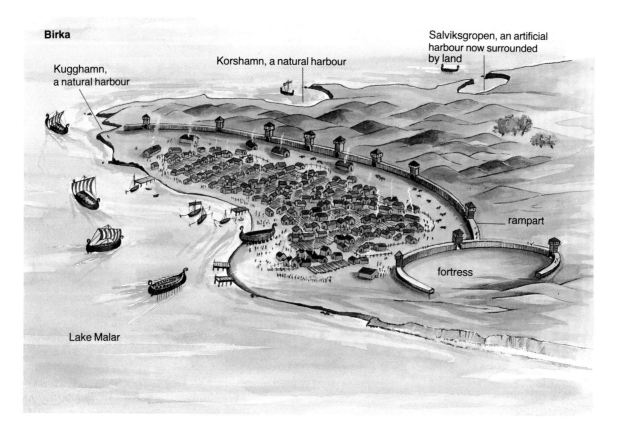

Birka

Kugghamn, a natural harbour

Korshamn, a natural harbour

Salviksgropen, an artificial harbour now surrounded by land

rampart

fortress

Lake Malar

This is Birka today. The shape of the land has changed because the level of the lake has fallen, but the line of the town wall is still clear to see.

As the Vikings travelled further they traded more and more. There were more things to sell in the ports. The ports grew. As they grew more people came to them.

Craftsmen who made things such as jewellery and weapons moved into the towns to live. They set up permanent shops. The trading towns became richer. This meant other people might attack them. So the Vikings built walls around them, to keep them safe.

Birka became a port in about AD800. Soon it had 1000 people living there. People such as shoemakers and weapon makers moved in. Houses and shops were built. The houses were very like longhouses, set sideways on to the street in their own fenced gardens.

Viking crafts

Viking farming families made most of the things they needed, from tools to clothes. As time went on, though, there were more and more craftsmen who made particular things. Most of them set up shops wherever they wanted, but smiths usually worked on the edges of towns, because their furnaces might cause fires.

The craftsmen made things people could not make at home. They made decorated tools, swords and beautiful jewellery. Viking men and women wore brooches, rings and arm rings.

This is part of a harness for a horse, which was found in Denmark. It is about 2 cm long. The carving is very detailed. It was made from bronze which was then covered with a thin layer of gold. Only a very rich Viking would have been able to afford a harness like this.

Viking jewellery was very complicated to make. Brooches were made from pewter, silver or bronze and sometimes coloured stones or jewels. Some craftsmen made necklaces of amber, jet or coloured glass beads. They made dice and counters for board games from amber and jet, too.

Other craftsmen made shoes, boots, combs and other things from bone and horn. These were things that could be made at home, but some Vikings, if they had the money to spare, preferred to buy them. They bought them in towns or from traders who went from farm to farm selling goods.

These tools of a Viking blacksmith were found in Norway. Blacksmiths made weapons and tools. Many farmers would have bought tools like these, and then made and repaired their own weapons and tools on their farms.

This comb was made from the antler of a red deer. Antlers and other horns, as well as bone, were used to make combs, as well as pins, needles, spoons, game counters and dice.

The Vikings and trade

We know where the Vikings traded, because archaeologists have found things from other countries in Viking graves and towns. Carved runes and Viking sagas and histories also tell about trading journeys. Runes have been found carved in places including Greece and Turkey. People in other countries also talk about the Vikings coming to trade there.

When all this evidence is put together, it shows that the Vikings traded in all of the places shown on the map below.

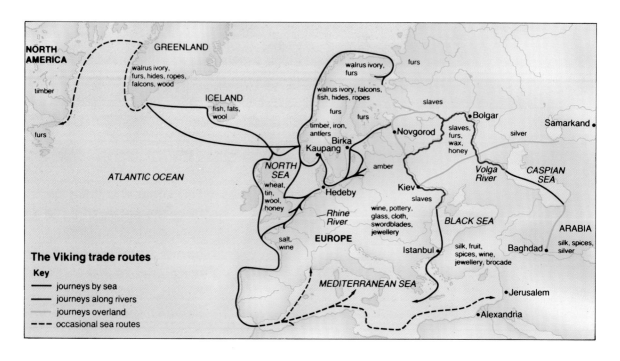

This is part of a collection of silver coins that were buried in a Viking grave at Skaill Bay, Orkney. Some of the coins are from Arabia. There were also large silver bars, brooches and arm and neck rings.

Viking traders needed scales. They traded by weight of silver, not with coins (coins were used to make weight). A merchant buried in Colonsay, in the Hebrides, was buried with his scales and a balance beam to hang them from.

The Vikings sailed to most of these places. They travelled mainly by sea, but they also sailed up rivers, including the Volga in Russia.

Ibn Fadlan, an Arab writer from the time, talks about the Vikings trading in Russia. He calls the Vikings who lived there the Rus: 'The Rus live on an island in the lake. They raid the Slavs and capture them. Then they sell them off to towns down the Volga. They also sell animal skins.'

Eventually the Rus settled down to farm, and the land became know as 'Rus land' and later Russia.

Transport

Whenever they could, the Vikings travelled by ship. They even carried their ships from one river to another, rather than travel any other way. Ships were quick, and could carry people and things. On long journeys the ships became the Vikings' homes. The mast could be let down and covered with the sail to make a tent, even at sea.

Sometimes the Vikings could not travel by water. Then they used the old Roman roads, which still crossed much of Europe. Sometimes they had to build their own bridges or roads.

These Viking skates were made from bone. They were tied to boots like the one on the left with strips of leather. Then the skaters pushed themselves along with poles.

The wagon on the left was found in the grave of a man in Oseberg, Norway. We know he was very important because he was buried with a ship (like the one in the diagram on page 38), and lots of jewellery and things which only a rich man would have (like the carved bed on page 23). Most wagons would not have had such fine carvings on them.

When travelling over land, the Vikings went on horseback if they could. When they could not ride the Vikings had to walk but they hated this, for it was slow, and it was hard work to carry things. If they could not travel by boat or horse, the Vikings preferred to do their travelling on the winter, when they could use skates or skis. In the *Orkney Saga* Earl Rögnvald says: 'I glide on skis, like the wind.'

Sledges were useful for carrying sick or old people, or taking heavy loads over the ice.

This tapestry shows the kind of wagons that the Vikings would have used.

Viking ships

The Vikings were very good sailors and shipbuilders. Most other countries had ships, but they were not as well **designed**, and people did not dare to travel out of sight of land in them.

The Vikings travelled well out of sight of land. They were very skilled in navigation (see pages 42 and 43).

They also went a long way up rivers. Their ships were narrow. They were made to sail in shallow water. Viking ships were also very light. The Vikings could carry them from one river to another.

A faering, the smallest Viking ship, was 6.5 m long and 1.4 m wide.

A knarr, used by traders or settlers, was 16.3 m long and 14.6 m wide.

The Gokstad ship looked like this. It was 23.3 m long and 5.2 m wide. The sail was made from strips of red and white cloth.

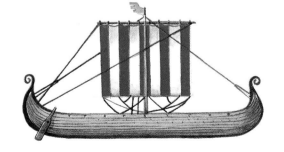

The Oseberg ship looked like this. It was 21.6 m long and 5 m wide.

A stone carving, found in Jarlshof, in the Shetlands, shows a Viking ship with a rudder at the back to steer with.

We know about Viking ships from carvings, sagas, and from ships that have been found as part of a burial.

This ship was found as part of a grave in Gokstad, Norway. There is a picture of what it would have looked like on page 38.

Building a Viking longship

Vikings built and repaired their ships in the winter, when they could not farm or raid. Ships were usually built in the open, but sometimes a boatshed was built around them, so that the men could work under cover.

Viking ships were built from oak, except for the mast, which was made of pine, so it could bend easily in the wind. The oars were oak too, about 5 m long. Most longships were about 20 m long. The keel was strongest if it was made from a single piece of wood. Some longships were too big to do this. King Canute had a longship about 60 m long.

The backbone of a Viking ship was its keel. The two curved end pieces were made separately, then fixed on. Then a heavy block was fixed to the keel. It had a hole in the top which the mast slotted into.

The sides were then put on, working from the bottom up (see the picture on the left). Then wooden planks were put from one side of the ship to the other to hold the ship in shape.

After this the ship was given a floor and holes for the oars.

The rudder which steered the ship was fixed on the right side, at the back.

Clinker building

After the first line of planks had been fixed in place with iron nails, the second line was fastened above them. The wedge shape allowed this second line to overlap the first. This is known as clinker-building. It makes the ship flexible so that it can sail on rough seas without breaking up.

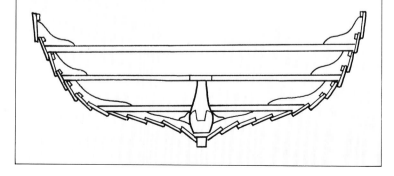

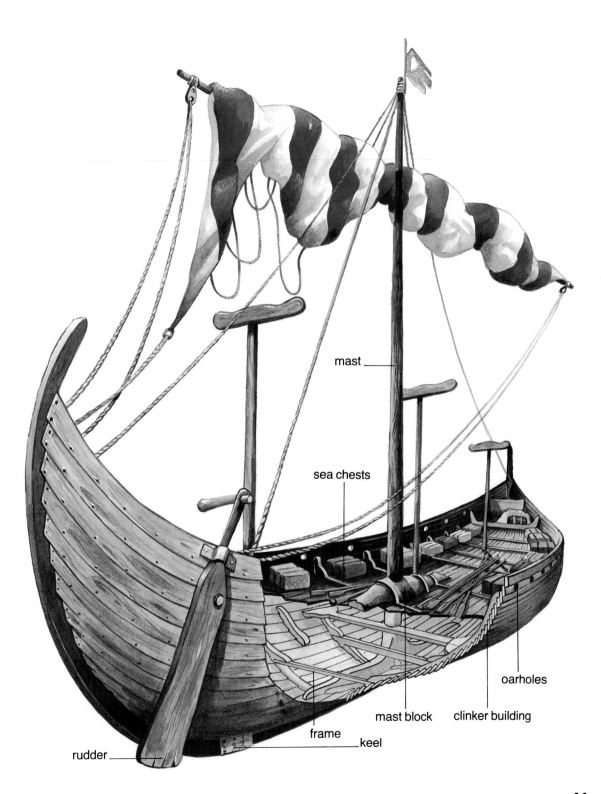

mast

sea chests

oarholes

mast block   clinker building

frame

keel

rudder

Sailing and navigation

Viking ships were home for their sailors, not just a way of travelling. Each Viking brought a chest with him, with clothes and weapons. He sat on it to row. Vikings only rowed when there was not enough wind to use the sail, or if their leader thought that they needed something to do!

The ship had a small space at each end that was boarded over. Food was stored there. The Vikings took butter, cheese, beer, water, meat, apples and nuts to eat. They also took dried, smoked and salted meat and fish. Cooking pots were stored here, and so were spare sails and tent poles. These were used to make tents if the Vikings were close enough to land to go ashore to sleep.

Each Viking had furs and a sort of sleeping bag to sleep in. If they were going on a long journey they had to sleep on board. Sometimes they even cooked on board, using a box of sand to light the fire in.

The Vikings were very good at navigating. How did they do it?

This carved stone from Gotland shows a ship with its sail up. Many people think that the criss-cross pattern on the sail is made by ropes fastened across to keep it from tearing.

A Viking weather vane. It would have been fixed at the top of the mast of the ship. Strips of metal would have been fastened to it to show how the wind was blowing.

The Vikings used the sun and stars to navigate. If these were hidden, they used lodestones, which were pieces of magnetic stone which swung to point north. They also told each other of journeys they had made.

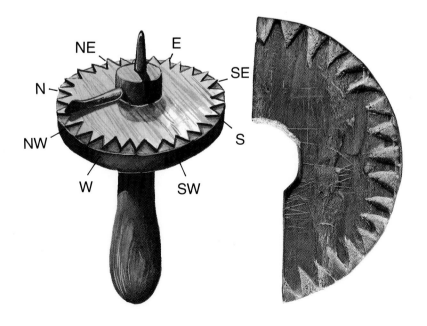

This broken piece of wood was found in Greenland. It was probably part of a bearing dial, used to navigate (see the drawing). The dial had 32 compass points. The sun cast a shadow and showed which way they were sailing. It was only useful if there was enough light to make a shadow.

Not just raiders

From AD780 onwards the Vikings travelled more and more. They were looking for places to trade with. They were also looking for countries that they could raid. Many Viking raids were made to steal animals and corn, to get food because they did not have enough at home. But, even if they mostly wanted food, the Vikings also took any valuables they could get. As they were often outnumbered by the people they attacked, the Vikings had to strike quickly, and hard.

Here are two pages from the *Codex Aureus*, an Anglo-Saxon book stolen by the Vikings in a raid on Kent. Later, an Anglo-Saxon earl bought it back.

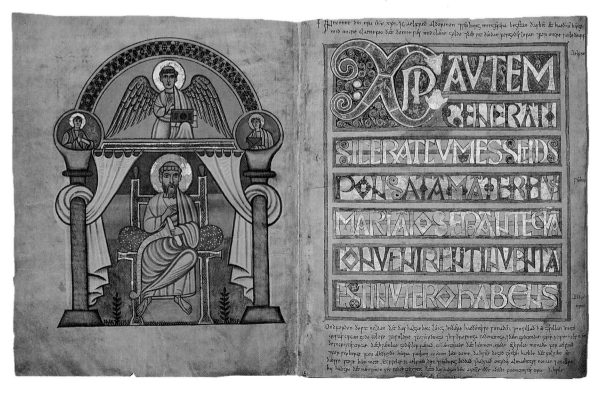

This is a picture of modern Norway. Norway did not have much good farmland. Sweden had many marshes and forests. Denmark had lots of sandy land where nothing would grow, so many Vikings moved to farm, not to raid. Viking graves, on Orkney and in other places, often having farming tools in them – but no weapons.

People were frightened by the Vikings. They saw them as cruel warriors. Sometimes the reason that Vikings left their homelands was more important than just for raiding, or even trading. They were looking for places to farm. Why?

When a Viking farmer died his eldest son took over the farm. The rest of his family had to move away. His sisters were often married anyway, but his brothers had to find land to farm. As time went on, there were more and more people looking for land to farm. There was not enough room for them in their homelands. They had to travel, to find somewhere else to settle.

Viking warriors

The Vikings were good warriors. They were often outnumbered by the people they attacked, so they relied on taking their enemies by surprise, and fighting so hard that people were scared of them.

How they fought depended on the number of their enemies and the land they were fighting on. They often began by throwing spears and firing arrows. Then they fought hand-to-hand with their swords or battle axes, or made a wall of their shields and fought from behind that.

Viking armour
Because they were farmers too, the Vikings had different types of armour, not just a single uniform. A Viking warrior would have some – but not all – of the weapons listed below:

a sword, made of iron

a battle axe, made of iron, with a blade about 24 cm across

a shield, made of wood, with an iron centre piece

a ring mail shirt or byrnie, often with as many as four layers of iron rings linked together, which could not be cut by a sword (These were very expensive. Only rich men could afford them and they were passed down from father to son.)

a metal pointed spear.

When they fought at sea, Vikings tied their boats together. The warriors would fight at the front of the ship, one at a time, until they were killed. The first warrior was often a fierce fighter, called a berserker. These warriors went mad to fight, often foaming at the mouth and fighting without armour. Their anger made them strong and frightening. No one really knows what made people like behave this, but it was something that fathers passed on to their sons. Often the enemy were so scared by the berserker that they ran away.

Swords were the most important Viking weapons. Some Vikings were buried with their swords. Other Vikings passed their swords on to their sons. Some were seen as magic, and had names, such as 'Leg Biter' or 'Adder'.

Many Viking helmets were made from leather, and fitted like a cap. Some had iron bands around the edge and across the top. Some were made all of iron, with a piece down over the nose to protect it.

The Vikings in England

The Vikings raided England for the first time in AD789, when they raided Dorset. From then on England was raided regularly by Vikings. The raids came at different times, in different places. Sometimes the English fought the Vikings, sometimes they gave them money, called **Danegeld**, to go away – but money was not always the answer. There were many different bands of Vikings, and paying one band off did not mean that you were safe from attack from any of the others.

Viking attacks were worst on weak parts of the country. There were some years, when Alfred the Great was King of Wessex, when the Vikings hardly raided at all. This was partly because Alfred made Wessex strong, but also because he and the Viking leader, Guthrum, agreed that the Vikings could settle in the part of England which is coloured orange and yellow on the map. The area was known as the Danelaw. The peace was always being broken, as one side or the other tried get more land.

This Viking cross is from Gosforth, in Cumbria, England. There are many places in England which have Viking crosses, especially in the parts of England where the Vikings settled. These areas are coloured yellow and orange on the map on page 49. The crosses are found in churchyards because many Vikings became Christians.

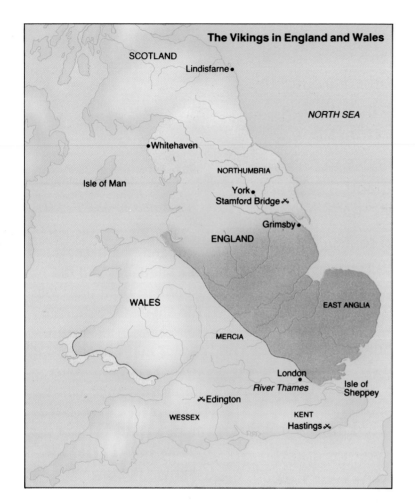

The Vikings in England and Wales

The fact that there were lots of different bands of Vikings meant that there was no peace from the raids. Even when a Viking, Canute of Norway and Denmark, was king of England there were still raids from Swedish Vikings. Canute had to pay them to go away, too. The raiding only stopped when William I became king in 1066.

This Swedish runestone tells of the Vikings being paid Danegeld by English kings – even Canute.

Scotland and Ireland

The Vikings raided Scotland and Ireland from AD795 onwards. The first raids were in the Orkneys, and then they worked around the Scottish coast and down to Ireland. The Viking raiders were mostly from Norway. They had a far bigger influence in these places than they did in England. They settled more rapidly. Some farms in the Orkneys and Shetlands have been dated to around AD800. They set up trade links with Norway. But the Vikings didn't just want to settle. They used the Scottish Islands and Ireland as stopping points as they moved further west.

The Scottish Islands had little trouble from other Viking bands, but the Vikings in Ireland had problems with Danish Vikings and the Irish. They moved out in about AD902, and went to Scotland, or the Isle of Man, but were back by AD917. Their stopping points became trading ports, and they began to settle and farm. They still were not accepted by the Irish, as battles, like those at Tara and Clontarf (see the map on page 51), show.

Lots of Vikings settled in Scotland, the Orkneys, the Shetlands and the Hebrides. Until the 1400s the Shetlands belonged to Norway. This picture shows the festival of Up-Helly-Aa in Lerwick, in the Shetlands, which takes place on the last Tuesday in January. A Viking ship is dragged through the town streets and then set alight to celebrate the beginning of the New Year.

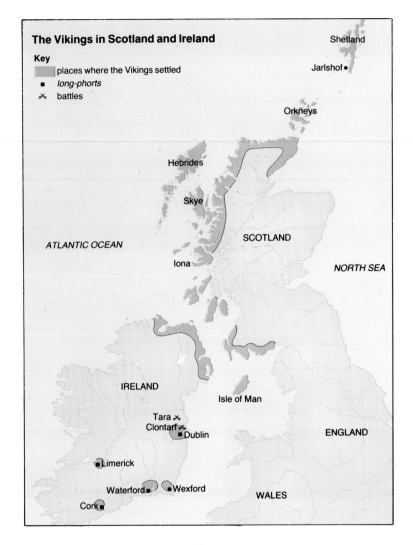

The Vikings in Scotland and Ireland

Key

places where the Vikings settled

■ *long-phorts*

⚔ battles

Shetland

Jarlshof •

Orkneys

Hebrides

Skye

ATLANTIC OCEAN

SCOTLAND

Iona

NORTH SEA

IRELAND

Isle of Man

Tara ⚔
Clontarf ⚔
■ Dublin

ENGLAND

■ Limerick

Waterford ■ ■ Wexford

Cork ■

WALES

The Vikings stayed put, despite Irish resistance, and were not driven out until 1100, when their biggest port, Dublin, was taken over by the Normans. The Normans were already ruling England, and were descended from Danish Viking bands!

This is part of a wall from Viking Dublin. It is made of wattle and daub, mud stuck on woven sticks. It was built in about AD950.

France and the Mediterranean

The Vikings behaved in the same way in France and the Mediterranean as they did in England, Scotland and Ireland. They raided and they traded. They raided monasteries, where possible. This was because monasteries were places where there would be plenty of food and treasure stored up. Also, the monks were peaceful men, and less likely to resist than other people.

The Vikings went around the coast of Europe, and as far up the rivers as they could.

This is a picture of Arab **Muslim** soldiers. The Arab armies in Spain managed to defeat the Vikings at Cordoba in AD844. The Vikings then left the Spanish Muslims in peace.

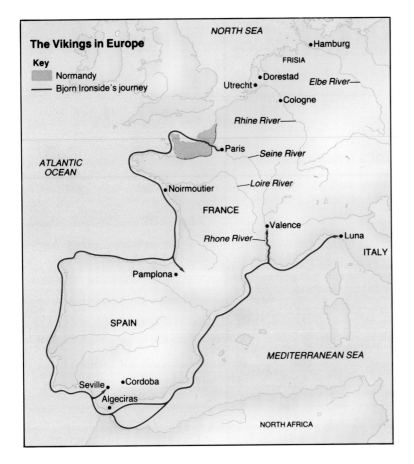

The Vikings in Europe

Key

Normandy

Bjorn Ironside's journey

This map shows the journey made by one Viking band, led by Bjorn Ironside, in AD859. They were driven out of their settlement on an island near Paris and worked their way around the coast of Spain into the Mediterranean, looting as they went, and stopping for the winter. They then went back to France, landing there in AD862.

The Vikings were a problem all over Europe, especially in France. The French kings paid Danegeld at first, like the English. Then King Charles the Simple of France did what Alfred had done in England. He gave the Vikings land. He made the Viking Rollo king of Normandy. Rollo was the great-great-great-grandfather of William the Conqueror, who became king of England in 1066.

This picture shows what a monk thought a Viking attack on a European city was like.

New lands to the west

The Vikings from Norway moved further and further west, looking for new lands to farm. They were also looking for new places to trade with, and for adventure. They reached Iceland in about AD860, and quickly settled there. There were Irish monks living there, but they left, for fear of the Vikings.

Their next stop was Greenland, seen in AD920 by a Viking blown off course between Norway and Iceland. It was first visited by Eric the Red, in AD980, who had been thrown out of Norway, and was then thrown out of Iceland too. Greenland was not really settled until around AD985. The 25 ships that went to settle took animals, corn and other things with them. As the years passed, the weather got colder. It got too cold to grow food. By 1500 Greenland was empty.

This is a picture, from an Icelandic book, of men catching a whale. The Vikings in Iceland wrote down the sagas and histories, on animal skin, in ink, in the long winters.

This is a reconstruction of L'Anse aux Meadows, where the Vikings may have settled. The *Vinland Saga* says America was first seen by Bjarni Herjolfsson in about 985, but he did not land. Lief Erikson landed there, and spent the winter. The sagas say that the Vikings tried to settle in America, but had trouble with the Indians, who they called 'skraelings'.

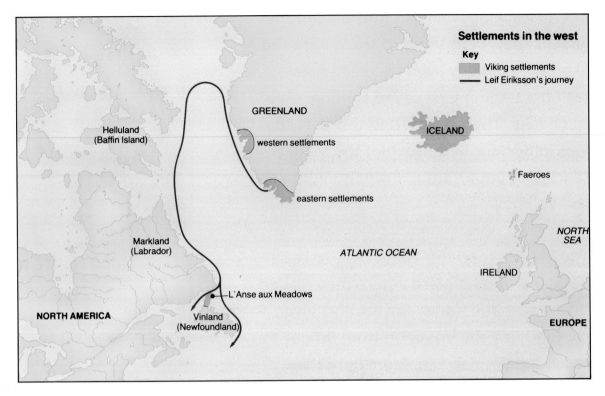

Settlements in the west

Key
Viking settlements
Leif Eiriksson's journey

GREENLAND

Helluland
(Baffin Island)

western settlements

ICELAND

Faeroes

eastern settlements

Markland
(Labrador)

ATLANTIC OCEAN

NORTH
SEA

IRELAND

L'Anse aux Meadows

NORTH AMERICA

Vinland
(Newfoundland)

EUROPE

People who read the *Vinland Saga* wanted to show that the Vikings reached America. They even faked evidence. A runestone, found in 1898, was shown to be a fake in 1958. The Vinland map, supposed to be a Viking map, was found in 1965. It was a fake, too. Then an arrowhead was found in a Viking grave in Denmark, made from a stone only found in America. This, and evidence from L'Anse aux Meadows, suggests that the Vikings did reach America.

If you look at the distances on the map, it seems sensible to think the Vikings reached America. They had already sailed all the way from The Scottish Islands to the Faroes, from the Faroes to Iceland and from Iceland to Greenland.

Trade routes to the east

The first Vikings reached Russia in about AD860. They went there to trade with the Slavs who already lived there. The Slavs had set up a trading port called Ladoga, on a huge lake. The Vikings used this port too. It was important because it let the Vikings reach two important rivers – the Volga and the Volkhov.

The Vikings used the Volga river to reach Bolgar, a trading place where they traded slaves, furs and honey for silk and silver. They could follow the Volga on from Bolgar to reach the Caspian Sea. From here they travelled by camel to Baghdad, where they could also trade for silk and silver, and for spices.

The second river that the Vikings could use was the Volkhov, which took them to Novgorod, which was a port that they set up. From here they could follow the River Dneiper to Kiev, and then to the Black Sea. Although it was a dangerous journey, the Black Sea took them to Istanbul, were they traded for wine, silk and jewellery.

This runestone is in Broby, Sweden. A woman put it up in memory of her husband. It says he visited Jerusalem and died in Greece. Thorfinn the Mighty, who ruled the Orkneys, went on journeys to England, Rome and Germany.

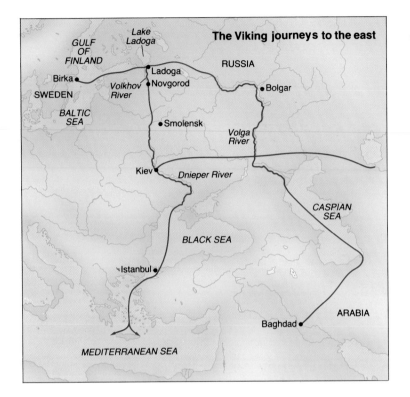

The Viking journeys to the east

Key

—— Viking trade routes

The Vikings travelled a lot in the area that we call Russia. The people there were called Slavs, and they often fought with each other. The Vikings, in their *Russian Chronicle*, say that they first went there because they were asked to send the Slavs a strong leader. A Viking called Rurik from Sweden took over and set up a trading port at Novgorod.

The Slavs and traders from other countries called the Vikings the Rus, which is how Russia got its name.

Many Vikings went home after such a long and dangerous voyage, but some stayed in Istanbul, to work as guards for the emperor there. One of these men went home to become Harald Hardrada, King of Norway. He was one of the people who tried to become king of England in 1066. He was defeated by William the Conqueror, who was descended from another Viking family.

Religion changes

The Vikings had lots of gods but, as time went on, more and more Vikings became **Christians**. Why?

Some Vikings became Christian because most of the people they traded with were Christian. Some Christians would only trade with other Christians.

Some Vikings became Christian because they had to. Olaf Tryggvason, king of Norway, came to Orkney in about AD995. He had more ships and men than Earl Sigurd, who ruled Orkney. He said that he would put Orkney 'to the sword and to fire' unless Sigurd and everyone else became Christian. They did.

This altar-piece from Denmark shows the baptism of Harald Bluetooth in about AD960. Many Vikings were converted to Christianity. Some were converted by force, like Guthrum in England. Some, like Rögnvald Kali in Orkney, were willing converts.

Many Vikings added Christianity to the old religion. In Colonsay, in the Inner Hebrides, a man was buried in the old way, but with stones with crosses cut into them as well.

Some Vikings became Christian because they really believed. Thorfinn the Mighty from Birsay, Orkneys, was one of these. So was Rögnvald Kali, who build the Cathedral of St Magnus in Kirkwall, in the Orkneys.

This is a smith's mould for making charms. The smith who owned it was making charms in the shape of a cross and in the shape of Thor's hammer. This shows that Christianity and the old Viking religion existed side by side for a while.

A stave church in Borgund, Norway. 'Stave' means built with upright planks of wood. It was begun in the 12th century, but finished in the 13th century. Despite the fact that it was finished after the Viking age, it still has Viking decoration.

End of the Vikings?

This is the Cathedral of St Magnus, Kirkwall, Orkney. The first Cathedral to be built here was built by the Viking Rögnvald Kali, and painted inside with bright colours. The walls were hung with tapestries or the sails from Viking ships.

The Vikings did not suddenly die out, or all get killed in battle. Instead, they settled into the places they had gone to, and became part of those countries. In some places they had to change their ways a lot to fit in. Rollo and his Vikings in Normandy did this. In places which were deserted when the Vikings came they changed their ways less. In Shetland people spoke a language called Norn, which was like the language of the Norwegian Vikings, until the 19th century.

In England the Vikings changed to fit in. They also added Vikings ways. Many English words came from the Vikings, including 'bread', 'sky', 'egg' and 'happy'.

The map opposite shows places with Viking place names, which tell us that the Vikings settled. Places with names ending in –by, –thorpe, –toft or –wick were probably Viking settlements.

Shetland Islands

Orkney Islands

Hebrides

SCOTLAND

IRELAND

Dublin

Isle
of Man

WALES

ENGLAND

EAST
ANGLIA

London

Edington

Athelney

Southampton

Hastings

WESSEX

Glossary

Archaeologist: a person who excavates places where people lived in the past, to study them.

Artefacts: things that someone has made.

Christians: Christians believed the teachings of Jesus Christ.

Danegeld: money paid to make Vikings go away.

Designed: if you design something you work out how it will look, and how it will work.

Excavate: to excavate a place you dig it up, very slowly and carefully, one layer of soil at a time. You note down all the things you find, and exactly where you found them.

Muslims: Muslims believed the teachings of the prophet Muhammet.

Outlawed: a person who has broken the law, and has shown they will not obey the law. They cannot be helped by anyone else.

Runes: Viking writing, usually found on stones or bone. Runes are mostly made up of straight lines.

Sagas: Viking stories which tell us about Viking life and history, but they have been made up in places to make things exciting. We cannot believe all they say.

Smithy: a place where iron is heated and made into weapons or tools.

Things: Viking parliaments where laws were made and arguments were sorted out.

Some important dates

789   First Viking raid on England, on Dorset.

793   Viking raid on the monastery of Lindisfarne, an island off the north-east coast of England.

795   Vikings start to settle on the Scottish Islands, starting with Orkney.
Vikings begin to raid Ireland.

799   Vikings move into south-west France.

841   Dublin, in Ireland, becomes a Viking base.

845   Vikings burn Hamburg. They raid Paris but are paid not to burn it. They attacked towns in Spain, but are beaten by the Muslims.

851   Vikings spend the winter in England for the first time.

860   Vikings settle in Iceland.

860s   Vikings raid Italy and north Africa, trade in Russia.

886   Vikings given and settle in the Danelaw in England.

911   Rollo the Viking becomes king of Normandy.

920   Vikings find Greenland.

982   Eric the Red settles in Greenland.

985   More Viking settlers move to Greenland.
Vikings find America.

1002   Leif Erikson finds Newfoundland.

1017   King Canute rules Denmark, Norway and England.

1035   Canute dies, Anglo Saxons end up ruling England.

1066   William the Conqueror takes England.

Index